Father Damien, Loving Neighbor

by

Sister Mary Pelagia Litkowski, O.P.

Illustrated by

Students of Mrs. Judy Rupar,
3rd and 4th Grade Teacher at
St. Michael Elementary School
Fremont, Michigan

Art Fettig's

Growth Unlimited Inc.

Dedicated To Sharing Positive Living Concepts With Children

36 Fairview, Battle Creek, MI 49017
Phone 1-800-441-7676 (616) 965-2229
Fax (616) 965-4522

Growth Unlimited books are available at quantity discounts with bulk
purchase for educational, business or sales promotional use.

Manufactured in the United States of America

Design, Layout and Typesetting

by

*Paula
Hopkins*

Library of Congress
Catalog Number 94-077541
Sister Mary Pelagia Litkowski, O.P.
Father Damien, Loving Neighbor

ISBN 0-916927-20-9

"AIDS is the leprosy of today. Father Damien could well be named the patron of those who are suffering from AIDS."

*** From a homily given by Father Ron Gronowski while pastor of St. Francis Church in Traverse City, Michigan

In our research for this book we discovered that the word "leper" is hurtful to those survivors of Hansen's disease (leprosy).

This was brought to our attention first by Irene W.Y. Letoto at the Damien Museum and Archives in Honolulu. She put us in touch with Ann and Makia Malo.

Makia is a survivor. Blind from leprosy at age 30, unable to read Braille because he has no feeling in his hand, Malo enrolled in the University of Hawaii when he was 37. Seven years later he received his B.A. in Hawaiian Studies. Makia Malo is a gifted story teller, public speaker and poet.

Our thanks to these wonderful people who helped us avoid being hurtful to others.

Dedication
In thanksgiving

To Father Donn Tufts for showing our school children how much God loves them.

And

To all my relatives and friends who prayed for the successful completion of this book.

Imprimatur
Given by
Most Rev. Robert J. Rose
Bishop of Grand Rapids
Thursday, June 9, 1994

Preface

My aim in this little story is to present a word profile made up of fact and fiction depicting an appealing role model for young or old whom we might imitate in whatever circumstances God has placed us. May the examples given here help readers to translate into action the same kind of Christ-like love and compassion Father Damien practiced in his short life.

Those wishing historical and chronological information about Father Damien may find it in any of the sources listed in the bibliography at the end of this work.

Molokai became a lovely little village.
Abigail Noirot

Father Damien, Loving Neighbor

Call me Mikai. I am one of the thousands of people afflicted with leprosy banished from my home and destined to spend the rest of my life on the island of Molokai. I want to tell you how Father Damien de Veuster proved himself to be the most loving neighbor anyone could ever have.

Never will I forget the day I realized I had leprosy after I went to the doctor to see about the strange sores on my body. There was no way I could escape being sent to Molokai, in the Hawaiian Islands. I tried to hide, but police hunted me down until they found me. When my parents learned that I had been found, they came to bid me good-bye before the ship would sail for Molokai. Sad farewells were said and I was soon on the ship.

Mournful thoughts filled my mind. I was young, not quite twenty, and had so many plans for my future. What would life be like on Molokai? I knew that Father Damien, a fairly young man, healthy and strong, had gone some time before to work for the patients there. I wondered if he would remember me, whom he had known in Puna. Knowing that he would be in Molokai lessened my fears. Then my thoughts were interrupted by the dismal sight before me. The crying and the painful screams I heard all around me filled my heart with such pity I almost forgot my own sorrow.

We had been told that we would receive all possible care in the hospital which had been built there. "Time will tell," I told myself, "I must not borrow trouble. Surely God will provide."

After a long voyage, we reached Kalaupapa, the landing site. We were received by Father Damien himself and many of the inhabitants. They gave us a hearty welcome. For most of us this eased the pain of being exiled. I especially was gratified to see that Father did recognize me. At first he registered surprise. Then he called my name, "Mikai, Mikai! Do not be afraid. You will soon be a part of our family. We will do our best to make you happy."

He clasped both my hands. He showed no fear of touching me. Then he moved from one person to another giving each the same loving welcome he had given me.

We all felt welcome.   Christine Carson

Christine Carson

Meeting a friend named Waku

Waku, one of the young men who was among those who greeted us, introduced himself to me. He told me life would not be so bad as we feared it might be.

"I will tell you much about our Kamiano (Damien) that will calm your fears," he assured me. "You will soon see that he can do anything. If there is something that needs to be done and you can't do it, tell him. He will do it." That was not news to me. I told Waku that Father Damien had been our pastor in Puna before he left for Molokai.

"Then, Mikai," he said, "you must know how the good of God's people always comes first before anything he needs or wants for himself. When he first came there was no place for him to live. The sight of our wretched huts here in Kalawao made him forget that. He slept under that pandanus tree." He said this as he pointed to the tree.

"It did not matter that he would have to fight the many kinds of bugs that would be crawling over him. His first concern was the building of cottages for the people whom he already considered his *family.*

He called on those of us who were able to help him to do the building. While we waited for the lumber he ordered from Honolulu, we chopped down trees from the hills and dragged them into the village."

Soon we all had a place we could call home. I began to notice that the people were not so unhappy as I expected them to be. Father was so sociable and lovable, so jovial and full of laughter, that they were very relaxed, especially when he was around. He visited everyone often. "His laughing, jokes, and funny remarks kept them laughing, too," Waku said.

But Father could get angry. Waku told me how depressed many could get. They would try to seek relief by drinking pain-killing intoxicating drinks which they concocted themselves.

"Sometimes," Waku remembered, "Father found them taking part in one of their drunken gatherings. He soon cut those short. He ran into their midst brandishing a switch that speedily disbursed them. No one held this against him. They know he only has their good at heart."

"Whoever is dear to me, I reprove
and chastise." Revelations 3:19

I liked the little cottage Father gave me.
Abigail M. Noirot

Abigail M. Noirot

Mikai's Mission

One day after I was settled in the little cottage Father had shown me would be my home, he told me he would like to have me help him with his work for the children. Until then I had not known that he and those who were able, had built a home for orphan boys and one for girls.

"You have been well instructed in your Faith, Mikai. You will be able to do much for these children. Come with me tomorrow and see just what I'd like to have you do. Most important of all remember that they need love. Some of their parents have died here. Some have been forced to leave their children here." Father paused and spoke softly to me.

"You must impress on the minds of these children that they are God's special children. Let them know how much He loves them.

Tomorrow you will witness what I really do for them. I will entrust them to you. From time to time I will visit them. I have great confidence in you, Mikai." Father smiled at me and then continued.

"You may think you are unfortunate, but I am convinced that God has singled you out to be one of them so that you could understand their pain and help them bear the cross of physical suffering as well as mental suffering and of ostracism from society."

Meeting With The children

Father's confidence warmed my heart and gave me a sense of worth and mission. Here was something I could do for God and His children. I looked forward to the morrow. Our first visit was to be to the orphanage for boys. As we arrived the next morning, Father was surrounded by boys of all ages. They ranged from kindergarten age to those in their early teens.

Father greeted them all and tried to give to each the attention that was so eagerly sought. When all were seated on the floor, he took his place in his accustomed chair as they arranged themselves before him.

The boys eyed me with curiosity, and whispered to each other. Father lost no time in satisfying their interest. "Boys, this is Mikai, a friend of mine. He is going to be your friend, too. He will he having classes with you and telling you stories. He will even be playing games with you."

The children loved to see Father. Christine Carson

All clapped their hands on hearing the last promise. Father continued, "Remember what I promised to tell you the next time I came?" A chorus of talking began, which Father stopped by raising his hand and making sure they knew each would be called upon. "Here, here! Raise your hands and you will have a chance to talk."

Each boy's recollection went on something like this, "Yes, Rico?"

"Father, you said you were going to tell us about yourself when you were a little boy."

"Yes, Rico. What else? Manu?"

"You are going to tell us how you were lost when there was a big celebration in town."

"Oh, oh! And Pake?" asked Father.

"You said you saved a cow's life once. You're going to tell us how you did it."

Then he asked, "Anything else? Kamu?"

"You're going to tell us how you almost drowned once when you were skating on ice."

Then Father winked at me and said, "Just one more. Pedro?"

"You're going to tell us about one of the times when you were naughty."

"My, oh my! I wonder which of those times I was going to tell you."

This was followed by a chorus of laughter.

"I wonder if I can tell you all these things today. I'll try. If you still have questions about me when I was a boy like you are, or when I grew up, I'll answer them another time. O.K.?"

"Yes, Father," the boys agreed.

Receive instruction from His mouth and lay up His words in your heart." Job 21:22

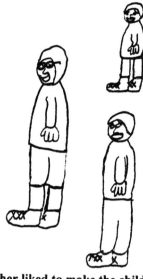

Father liked to make the children laugh.
Greg Oosterhouse

Greg Oosterhouse

Father's Story

*A*nd so Father began the story of his childhood. "In our family there were eight children. I was next to the youngest. My sister Mary, the baby of the family, died when she was fourteen. That made me the youngest.

But I didn't think I was the baby. I tried to do everything my brothers and sisters did, good or bad. They used to join hands and stretch themselves across the road on our way home from school. I always joined them," he continued.

"Once we happened to come to a turn in the road. A cart was coming toward us. We screamed and cleared the road as fast as we could, all except one of us. I was that one. The wheel of the cart hit me squarely in the head," Father told us.

Cries of "Oh, oh, Father!" came from the boys. "Did you get hurt bad?"

"Not really. I had a bump on my head where the wheel of the cart struck me. My back hurt a little bit." Father explained.

"What happened when you got home? Did your mother or father scold you?" asked one of the boys.

Father Damien smiled and responded, "They told me never again to play that dangerous game. My mother said I better thank my good guardian angel for taking such good care of me."

More Guardian Angels

"Another time my guardian angel kept me from drowning. I used to love to go skating on ice when I was

9

growing up at our home in Belgium," Father began. "I could beat almost anybody. One day I was a little too smart. I hit some thin ice and I heard it begin to crack. That scared me.

Quick as a wink, I asked my guardian angel to help me. Just as I was about to break through the ice I stretched toward the thick ice and reached it just in time. That saved me from sinking into deep water. What do you think I learned from that?"

One of the boys answered, "That you had to be careful where you skate?"

"Yes, Miko. What else?" Father asked.

"That your guardian angel helped you," Joni replied.

"Good for you, Joni. God has given each one of you a guardian angel to watch over you and keep you safe. What does that tell you about God, Miko?"

And Miko replied, "That God loves us."

Father nodded. "You have learned your lesson well. And why does God love you, Roni?"

"He made us." Roni replied.

"O.K. You are His children," Father explained, "and He will always love you and care for you. I remember sometimes when I did something wrong. One time I thought I was doing something good. It made my mother and father worry about me and caused them lots of trouble.

I thought I would be just like the saints my mother read about to us. I was only five years old. Our whole family was having a wonderful time at the Flemish fair. They were having fun, playing games, eating and drinking. I sneaked away from the crowd."

"Where did you go?"

"I went to the church to pray," Father replied. "No one knew where I was. They looked all over and could not find me."

"But you went to pray, Father." Roni protested.

"It was not right to cause everybody to worry about me."

"How did they find you?" asked Miko.

"My grandfather guessed where I might be. He went to the church. They followed him. There I was hiding under the pulpit." Father Damien laughed.

"Did you get punished for that?" questioned Joni.

"I wasn't punished for wanting to pray, but my mother told me how they worried about me," explained Father. "She said that I should never go anywhere without letting them know where I was going. I didn't always do what my mother wanted me to do, she kept reading to us about saints and hermits. I thought we should be like them. One day when I was a little older, I talked some of my schoolmates into being like hermits.

On the way home we went into the woods and stayed there praying and thinking about God until night time. Our families were so worried. They thought something terrible had happened to us. When we finally got home, we all got the spankings we deserved. I never tried that again," Father said firmly.

Galloping Horses

"Father, you told us some of the naughty things you did, but they were things you thought were good. Did you ever do anything you knew was bad?" Kim asked him.

"Oh, yes, Kim. I used to get into arguments and fights with other kids. I knew that was bad and later I would tell them I was sorry.

Sometimes we did things that really kept our angels busy. It was fun to jump on wagons going through our village and scare horses by throwing pebbles at them. They were soon galloping wildly, this made the drivers angry and we had to get off the wagons fast if we didn't want them to give us a good whipping.

One time we climbed onto a wagon that was standing still. We thought the driver was sleeping. He wasn't. He was ready for us and had friends hiding who were waiting for us. As soon as one of my friends threw a pebble at the horse, the driver pulled in the reins to keep him from galloping away.

We got what was coming to us. I didn't have to get spanked at home that time," Father said.

"Why didn't you, Father?" Miko asked.

Father Damien told them, "I didn't go home 'til late that night. Everyone thought I was lost."

11

"Why? Where did you go?" one of the children asked.

"I remembered stories my mother told me about how criminals who were being hunted would be safe if they hid in a church near the altar.

They would not leave until they got a promise that they would not be punished. I hid in the church. No one thought of looking for me until my uncle remembered how the family found me in church praying when everyone else was having a good time at the town fair. When they found me this time, they begged me to come home, but I wouldn't go until my father promised I would not be punished."

A Sick Cow

"What would you like to hear now?" Father asked.

"Father, tell us, how did you save that cow's life?" pleaded Roni.

"Oh yes," answered Father Damien, "we have time for just one more story about me. One of our neighbors, a dear old lady, was afraid her cow was going to die. I was there when the veterinarian told her there was no hope. The cow would die.

I felt so sorry for the lady. That cow was all she had. She asked a butcher to come and see what he could do. After the butcher worked on the cow for some time he looked so tired.

I told him I could do what he was doing and he could go home. He was glad to be relieved and I stayed all night with the cow. By morning the cow was much better and we knew it wouldn't die."

"You were like a doctor, weren't you, Father? That's why you can help everyone here now, isn't it?"

"You could say that, Karo," Father replied. "God gets us ready for the work He wants us to do and helps us do it. Now it is time to go. Before Mikai and I leave, let's say a little prayer to thank God for all He is doing for us. Tomorrow Mikai will come to visit you and teach you many things. Ready?"

Father Damien prayed, "Dear God, we praise You. We bless You. We thank You for loving us and for all You are doing for us. Good-bye. Don't get into trouble."

"Good-bye, Father. Thank you, Father."

All crowded around Father to give him good-bye hugs. As Waku had told me, Father did not hesitate to accept their hugs and returned them while responding, "You're very welcome."

> *"Take to heart these words which I enjoin on you today. Drill them into your children."*
> *Deuteronomy 6:7*

Father often walked in the cemetery, praying and thinking.
Steven Zielinski

Father played games with the children.
Darrel Carson

Darrel Carson

Love One Another

I had been listening intently as Father told these stories about himself. I thoroughly enjoyed the boy's reactions and knew that I was going to love working for them.

After that Father came off and on to see how I was doing with his boys. They always looked forward to his visits and hated to see him leave even though they did see him at Mass and at meals.

He spent other times with them, even playing games with those who were still able to play. A few of the orphans were not sick and those who were suffering from leprosy were in various stages of the disease.

Time passed quickly and I learned much about what Father Damien was doing for these poor people. I knew he would do much for me when my great suffering came. I made up my mind I would help him as much as I possibly could until that time came.

Life was fairly easy when I saw Father going about his normal routine, serving his people. The children in the two orphanages were Father's delight. It was his contact with them, besides his hours of prayer before the Blessed Sacrament and his celebration of the Liturgy of the Holy Eucharist that gave him the grace, strength and courage he needed to carry on his work of love.

In the cemetery near his home, he also spent much time meditating and praying. It was not long before I saw why Makua Kamiano, as Waku called him, needed these helps.

A new way of life

The first time Father took me through the hospital, I was filled with horror. I thought, "Is this what will happen to me?" Father had tried to prepare me for the sights I would see.

But no words could clearly describe what I saw. There were human beings who no longer looked like human beings, because of decaying flesh. I wanted to run away. In spite of this I was fascinated by the way Father showed his love for them. His words encouraged me.

Father took me to visit patients.
Greg Oosterhouse

Greg Oosterhouse

"Hang in there, Mikai," he would say when we were alone. "God will help you. He will be your strength when you are weak. When I first saw these people wrapped in rags and lying in their huts, I could scarcely bear the sight and odor of their bodies. You see how smoking helps me. I've never encouraged smoking, but this stench overwhelmed me. I could never survive if I did not smoke."

So it was that Father's love brought some joy into the lives of these people and instilled in their hearts the assurance that God in His love for them would one day call them Home. They would be beautiful and free from all their suffering. When he preached, he made himself one of them. Sometimes he would say, "We lepers cannot suffer alone. We must help one another."

Little by little I became accustomed to my new way of life. I helped Father build coffins for the dead. Someone died almost every day. He could not let bodies be wrapped only in old, filthy blankets and lowered into shallow holes in the ground as had been done before he came. He conducted beautiful funeral ceremonies. For these the people sang and were filled with joy for those whom God had called Home, for whom pain and sorrow were no more.

" I give you a new commandment: Love one
another. Such as my love has been for you,
so must your love be for one another."
John 13:34,35

18

Father made sure no one went hungry. Greg Oosterhouse

Greg Oosterhouse

No One Went Hungry

I marveled at what one person could do for so many people. News of Father Damien's wonderful work began to spread. Help came to him for his people from far and near. Not only Catholics sent help, but Protestant ministers and doctors did their best to obtain from their flocks, supplies and money to send to him.

The Board of Health, which at first was slow to fulfill his requests, even began supplying him with the same allotment of food that was furnished for the people.

To make sure no one went hungry, Father set up a store of his own. He kept it filled with food and supplies sent to him from the Sisters of the Sacred Hearts and other friends. Instead of selling these supplies, he gave them away. He questioned no one, even though there were those who asked for more than they needed. He turned no one away. His supplies never ran out.

"...the Lord your God is... the Lord of
Lords... Who has no favorites, who executes
justice for the orphan and the widow, and
befriends the alien, feeding and clothing him.
So you, too, must befriend the alien..."
Deuteronomy 10:17-19

Each day found many lined up
to receive free food and supplies.
Kay Witt

Kay Witt

Giving Comfort

One day I accompanied Father on one of his visits to the little hospital for children which Waku and others had helped him build. It was filled with patients and some of the able-bodied, who had leprosy, were helping him.

As Father lifted the blanket that covered one of the little girls, the sight that met my eyes almost knocked me over. Here was a child whose face no longer looked like a face. Her skin was black and smeared with a strange, gray pus oozing over it.

That face smiled after Father spoke his greeting, "How's my little Maria today? We have come to bring you some comfort. It will make you feel a little better." He lifted her head and gave her a little drink from the cup of milk he had for her.

His words caused her to smile her thanks. I could not help thinking that Father was taking the place of the parents who had been forced to leave their children here. He really was father and mother to them.

Soon I was helping Waku lead prayer sessions for all who could attend. The beauty of their prayers and singing showed how happy their Makua Kamiano had made them.

The chapel, too, was filled every Sunday. Many who were able came during the week for the Masses Father celebrated then.

*"We do not lose heart, because our inner
being is renewed each day even though our
body is being destroyed at the same time."*
II Corinthians 4:16

Father took me to see patients.
Darrel Carson

Darrel Carson

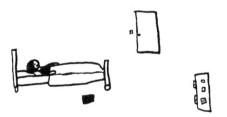

Some patients could not leave their beds.
Adriana Buck

Adriana Buck

Father confessed his sins to Father Modeste from the canoe.
Greg Oosterhouse

Greg Ooster house

A New Helper, An Old Friend

One day Waku and I joined a group of patients who were headed toward the shore. A small ship had anchored there and we knew more of the afflicted were about to leave it. Father Damien joined us. We eagerly awaited the moment when we would do our best to lessen the heartbreak of those who would spend the rest of their lives on Molokai.

Father Modeste, Father Damien's Provincial, was on board. The captain forbade him to leave the ship. Father got into a canoe and started paddling toward the ship.

"No one from the island comes aboard," shouted the captain. "Orders is orders. The Board of Health forbids it."

Then we saw something which made us admire our beloved pastor more than ever. From the canoe, in the presence of all these people aboard the ship and on shore, Father confessed what he considered his sins to Father Modeste and received absolution from him.

As the ship pulled away, Father and all on shore who were able, waved good-bye. We began to welcome the new arrivals. Suddenly, I stopped in my tracks and caught Waku by the arm. "Waku," I whispered, "Waku! I see someone I knew at home!"

Waku looked where I was pointing. There among those who had just come ashore was Maia, a young lady whom I knew before I was shipped off to Molokai. She had been a good friend of mine. I thought I would never see her again. She looked sad and forlorn as I had felt the day I landed on Molokai.

"Maia! Maia!" I called and hurried to meet her. As soon as she saw me, the sadness in her expression was replaced by joyful recognition.

"Oh, Mikai, I'm so glad to see you! I'm so glad to see you!" That was all she could say.

Maia meets Father Damien

I introduced her to Waku. Soon we were telling her that life would not be so miserable as she had expected it would be, thanks to Makua Kamiano and his beloved people. I called Father over. I was sure he had known her before he left Puna. He recognized her immediately.

"Welcome, Maia, welcome!" was his hearty greeting. "You will receive the help you need here. You will be able to serve your poor, suffering brothers and sisters. You will be able to do much for them. I remember you well, Maia. God has work for you to do here."

Maia seemed doubtful. "Thank you, Father, for your kind words. But how can I help when I, too, am one of the sufferers?"

"Never fear, Maia. This illness takes some time before it makes the victim helpless. You were a well-trained nurse and you were faithful in the practice of your Faith. We need you. As you relieve the sorrow and pain around you, yours will be easier to bear."

Every ship brought more patients. Clint Kempf

Clint Kempf

After welcoming everyone, Father led us all to the chapel where we thanked God for their safe arrival. Then he showed where each was to be housed. Maia was well impressed, "I had no idea Molokai would be like this. What a lovely village!" She exclaimed.

I told her all that Waku had told me, that it had not always been like this before Makua Kamiano came. In a shorter time than it would take to tell, Maia knew what Father and his helpers had done to transform those miserable shacks into neat little cottages.

She learned how Father had made possible the piping of water from a spring in the mountains, and how after that the people had good water to drink, to bathe and to wash their clothes.

Maia asked many questions as time went on. She learned more and more about the sacrifices, difficulties and even opposition from people who were jealous of Father's popularity and the glory and honor that the name Damien was receiving from far and near.

Our hearts ached for him when we heard of lies that were spread about his character. We knew that his morals were beyond reproach. He was forgetful of himself and thought only of what would help his people. He never made us suffer because of any hurt he was experiencing.

He had a fiery and fearless nature, but only let it show whenever his requests or plans for the good of the people were opposed. It showed whenever he broke up scandalous dances and wild, drunken parties that were carried on by those who insisted that "in this place there is no law."

"How can Father carry on in spite of the obstacles he has had to face?" Maia wanted to know. "What about the odor that comes from so many decaying bodies, the foul breath, the terrible sights? How can he eat with them, smoke the same pipe with them, let them touch him? Aren't those things too much for him to bear?"

My answer convinced her! "But he loves them and his strength comes from above. I know. I've seen him prostrate himself before the Blessed Sacrament for long periods of time. He prays much each morning before his day's work begins. God's love for His people flows through Father Damien."

27

Waku agreed with what I said and told Maia that Father admitted that he could not do it without the grace, strength and courage that God gives him through prayer and the celebration of the Holy Eucharist.

"To Him whose power now at work in us can do immeasurably more than we can ask or imagine----to Him be glory." Ephesians 3:20, 21

Love and Puppies

Maia's service as a nurse proved indispensable. She also began teaching catechism classes and became a prayer leader. With Waku we became quite a team. We worked hard and little by little we began to feel the effects of the leprosy which was in our systems. Father Damien showed his love and concern for us all the more.

The time came when Father himself began to feel symptoms of leprosy. This did not surprise him or us. It only made him rejoice to think that now he could be even more closely united with his people.

What could we do but follow his example? Just as he was doing, we could keep on working for the people as long as we were able.

Father knew he had leprosy when his feet felt nothing while in scalding hot water.
Leon Slater

"How I love to have Father visit my class, Mikai," Maia told me not long after she had begun to instruct the little ones. "They're not the least bit afraid. They answer him without hesitation. They vie with one another to ask him to pray for something or someone.

I laughed so hard when Jedi asked him if God would let him have a puppy when he gets to Heaven. Father said 'Jedi, if you want a puppy when you get to Heaven you'll have one.' That satisfied him. When Father is ready to leave these children flock to him. Each one tries to be the first to give him a good-bye hug."

That reminded me of a time when Father asked the children during the intercession time at Mass if there was anything or anyone they wanted us to pray for. One of the boys said, "For Father and for my puppies."

"Let the little children come to Me and do not hinder them. It is to such as these that the Kingdom of God belongs... Then He embraced them, placing His hands on them." Mark 10:14, 16

Maia helped much with the children.
Steve Morrison

Steve Morrison

Makua Kamiano Is One Of Us

Father kept saying, "We lepers," whenever he gave homilies at Mass. Maia asked me if Father, too, had leprosy. My answer caused her great concern. "We've heard from a lady who gets his meals that he has begun to notice some symptoms. Once he was soaking his feet in hot water. The water was scalding hot and he didn't feel a thing. That's a sure sign."

The water was scalding & Father's feet felt nothing.
Christine Carson

Christine
Carson

We wondered how soon it would be before Father would have to stop working. We could not tell because he kept on going as if nothing were wrong. He was still cheerful whenever any of us were with him. His jokes and laughter helped us all to forget our woes.

We marveled that he could be so light-hearted when he was so alone. He had been here a long time and no one had come for any length of time to help him.

"He must have his *down* moments," Maia remarked during one of our get-togethers. Waku agreed. "When I go strolling in the evening sometimes, I see him walking in the cemetery. He doesn't know anyone sees him. I've heard him crying and praying out loud."

'If two or more ask.. in My Name..'

"Why don't we pray that God will send someone who will stay with him and help him? You know Jesus said 'If two or more ask the Father for anything in My Name, He will give it.' " Maia suggested.

From that time on we prayed every day that someone would come to help our dear Kamiano, someone who would be a real friend. He needed someone who would understand him and share his concern for all of us here and help him in his work.

The day came when our prayers were answered. God sent a man named Joseph Dutton from America who had served as a soldier in the Civil War. We discovered later that he had led a wild life for some years. He reformed and tried the life of a Trappist brother and learned that this was not his calling.

In his travels he found an article in a Catholic paper about Father Damien and his work with those afflicated with leprosy. After studying more about Molokai, he felt that this was what God wanted him to do.

We saw Father Damien meet him as he left the ship that brought him to Molokai. Father looked so happy and greeted him warmly.

Father had Mr. Dutton live with him until they built a little house for him. To our Kamiano, he was Brother Joseph, and so that is what we called him.

Thank you God, for sending someone to help Father.
Christine Carson

Christine Carson

They became fast friends and Brother Joseph was a wonderful help to Father Damien. They were able to build more houses for the new patients coming to Molokai. They kept up with the building of coffins for the many people who were dying every day.

A Second Blessing

The news that Father Damien had leprosy spread like wild fire. Father Lambert Conrardy was a priest from Belgium, Father Damien's home land. He knew Father Conrardy and of his work with American Indians before his Bishop sent him to work in Hawaii.

When Father Conrardy heard how much Father Damien needed help, he wrote to Father asking him if he would like to have him come to help him. Father Damien was so delighted that he begged his Bishop to send Father Conrardy to assist him at Molokai. The Bishop sent him.

Here was another answer to our prayers! Father now had two special friends, one who could help him in his spiritual needs as well as with the work for his beloved patients.

"I lift up my eyes toward the mountains,
whence shall help come to me? My help is
from the Lord, who made Heaven and earth."
Psalm 121:1, 2

So Little Time

The day that we were dreading came sooner than we expected. For us it came too soon. It was the day the leprosy became noticeable on Father's body. This time it was more than the lack of feeling in his feet when he soaked them in scalding hot water.

The knowledge that he had leprosy was no surprise to our Kamiano. He had told the doctor who examined him he knew the day would come. Father was persuaded to go to Honolulu to the hospital in which a group of Sisters were caring for patients that were just beginning to suffer from leprosy.

We knew that Father would not be gone long. His love for his patients was too great to let him desert them without being sure that someone would take his place, to be there when he was no longer able to care for them, to carry on the work he had begun.

We were right. Soon he was back with us, working harder than ever. We saw day by day what leprosy was doing to him, what we ourselves would have to suffer one day. Sores appeared on his forehead and on his ears. His nose began to swell. Soon he had no eyebrows. He became more and more tired.

We tried to get him to slow down, but he would not. He said there was so much more to do, and he had so little time. "How soon do you think Father will be confined to his bed?" I asked Waku.

"It won't be long now, I'm sure," was his sad answer. "I've seen this happen to so many. It isn't long before they can hardly breathe, or even walk. Then they cannot leave their beds."

I had seen this, too, and wondered at Father's cheerfulness in spite of all he was suffering. "He is practicing what he has preached to all of us," Waku reminded me. "He is looking forward to the happiness he will have forever when God calls him Home. Remembering this helps me when I think of the time I will be suffering in the very same way."

"I give you My word, if you are ready to believe that you will receive what you ask for, it shall be done for you." Mark 11:24

The Bishop sent Father Conrardy to Molokai.
Joseph Gates

Gates
Joseph

**Father asked to be buried under the pandanus tree where
he had slept when he first came to Molokai.**
Matthew Rupar

Matthew Rupar

"God has heard my prayers."

The day came when Father Damien could no longer leave his bed. Waku, Maia and I kept on with our duties, but we visited him whenever we could. During our last visit he told us that soon some Franciscan Sisters would be coming to Molokai to care for the patients.

"Help me to thank God, my dear helpers," he begged. "God has heard my prayers. The Sisters will be able to care for my boys and girls better than I could ever do. I can die in peace. My work is done.

How I cried when our dear Kamiano died!
Heather Kuziak

Heather Kuziak

Thank you, Mikai, Waku and Maia for all you have done to help me, and to help God's dear children. When your time comes, and you can no longer work, Father Conrardy and Brother Joseph will see to your needs. We will meet again when God calls you Home. There we shall be happy forever and forever."

Maia could not hold her tears back, as Father said good-bye. He promised to pray for us when he was with God in Heaven.

By this time the bishop had sent another priest to help Father Conrardy once Father Damien could no longer carry on. Father Conrardy told us that Father Damien said he would die at the beginning of Holy Week. His prediction came true. He breathed his last, quietly and gently, peacefully smiling. I could not help hoping and praying that my death would be as happy and peaceful as his was.

"Precious in the eyes of the Lord is the death of His faithful ones." Psalm 116:15

Father preached to us during Mass.
Leon Slater

Waku heard Father cry when he walked
in the cemetery.   Abigail Noirot

Many patients came to Mass.
Greg Oosterhouse

There was a little hospital
that Father built.
Heather Kuziak

Our Beloved Kamiano

Father's funeral was just like those he had conducted for his patients. He was clothed in his priestly vestments. In his coffin he lay in state in the Church. His patients, his beloved *family* filed by him, their tears freely flowing.

His funeral Mass and procession were just like all their funeral Masses and processions. Father had asked to be buried under the pandanus tree where he had slept so many nights after his arrival in Molokai. There they laid him to rest.

So ends my little tale about one, who, I believe, proved himself the most loving neighbor anyone could ever have. My friends and I now await the day when we will join our beloved Kamiano and our own loved ones from whom we were snatched. There with them we will enjoy forever the peace and happiness which God has promised.

"This is My commandment: Love one another
as I have loved you. There is no greater
love than this: To lay down one's life for
one's friend." John 15:12-14

Highlights in the Life of Father Damien, SS.CC.

January 3, 1840	Born at Tremeloo, Belgium
January, 1859	Entrance into Congregation of Sacred Hearts Fathers
October 7, 1860	Final Vows as Brother of Sacred Hearts Congregation
March 19, 1864	Arrival at Honolulu with fellow missionaries
May 21, 1864	Ordination into the Priesthood at Cathedral of Our Lady of Peace in Honolulu
1864-1873	Service in Puna, Kohala and Hamakua
1873-1889	Labor among the sufferers on Molokai
April 15, 1889	Death of Father Damien
1936	Father Damien's body exhumed and returned to Belgium where his body lies in state in St. Joseph Chapel in Louvain
July 7, 1977	Father Damien declared "Venerable" by Pope Paul VI
1995	Beatification is tenatively scheduled for 1995 by Pope John Paul II.

Quotes from Father Damien's Letters and Conversations

"I consider myself an instrument in God's hands. How many times in the past have I been providentially led out of my way to little huts where I brought new life to old folks and prepared the dying for eternity... In spite of privations and misery, God often gives me consolations I never expected."

"My greatest happiness is to serve the Lord in these poor sick children, made outcasts by the rest of men. I'm trying hard to lead them along the road to Heaven."

"I find my greatest happiness is serving the Lord in these poor suffering children who have been rejected... Dear parents, dear brethren and friends, follow that same path so we may meet above... Pray very much for me."

"Our poor islanders are very happy when they see Kamiano (Damien) coming. And I, for my part, love them very much. I would gladly give my life for them as our Savior did. I don't spare myself when it's a question of going twelve or fifteen miles to visit the sick."

"I live always with seven or eight hundred lepers. I have filled a cemetery with the dead, and soon, for lack of space, we are going to have to dig up the first part and put coffins on top of one another."

"Ah! If you knew the beautiful music we have in my church!"

"...A doctor advised me to breathe some of my native air. Up to now neither our bishop nor I have found this advisable. What would become of my poor sufferers? No! I can always do a little good, I will remain at my post until death. We won't see each other here, but in Heaven."

"The wearier I am, the happier I feel."

"The sight of what souls have cost Jesus Christ ought to inspire us with the greatest zeal for the salvation of the whole world. We should give ourselves to all without exception, without reserve. The measure of our zeal should be that of Jesus Christ."

"I wouldn't be cured if the price of my cure was that I must leave the island and give up my work."

"From morning to night I am amidst heartbreaking, physical and moral misery. Still, I try to appear always joyful, so as to raise the courage of my patients. I present death to them as the end of their ills, if they will make a sincere conversion. Many see their last hour come, with resignation, and some with joy. Thus, in the course of this year, I have seen a hundred of them die in very good dispositions."

"How good God is, to have made me live long enough to see at this moment two priests at my side and the Franciscan Sisters at the Settlement! Now I can sing, *Nunc Dimittis* (Now Thou dost dismiss Thy Servant, O Lord). The work for the lepers is in good hands and I am no longer necessary. I am going to Heaven."

"How sweet it is to die a member of the Congregation of the Sacred Hearts of Jesus and Mary."

Some of the virtues modeled by the life of Father Damien

Faith -- Christian -- Belief in God or in someone or something open to question.

Hope -- Christian -- Trust, reliance.

Charity -- Christian -- Act of loving all people as brothers and sisters.

Obedience to God's Command -- Ancient Israel -- A standard of rules and regulations.

Humility -- Christian -- Freedom from pride or arrogance. State or quality of being humble in spirit.

Prudence -- Aristotle -- Practical wisdom and the ability to make the right choice in special situations.

Justice -- Aristotle -- Fairness, honesty, keeping promises.

Fortitude -- Aristotle -- Courage, guts. The strength of mind and courage to persevere in the face of adversity.

Temperance -- Aristotle -- Sex, food, drink, self-discipline, the control of all unruly human passions and appetites.

A Novena of Prayers to Jesus for help in living a virtuous life as inspired by the life of Father Damien

Day One For FAITH

Lord, let my _faith_ in You be unbounded just like Damien's faith in you.

Day Two for HOPE

Lord Jesus, give me _hope._ When despair raises its ugly head please let me remember the brave example that Damien gave us by being hopeful to the very end.

Day Three for CHARITY

O Lord, so often I think only of myself. Like Damien, help me to think of the _welfare of others_ first.

Day Four for OBEDIENCE

Yes, Lord, help me to _obey your laws_ in all ways as Damien strived to do throughout his lifetime.

Day Five for HUMILITY

Damien cared little for human praise and glory. "Praise God, not me." He said. Lord, I can do nothing without you. <u>Let me direct all praise and glory to you.</u>

Day Six for PRUDENCE

Oh Lord, give me the <u>wisdom</u> to choose what is best for my own spiritual welfare as Damien did so often in his life.

Day Seven for JUSTICE

Oh Lord, help me to seek <u>justice</u> for all, especially those in greatest need of our love and understanding just as Damien did for the afflicted at Molokai.

Day Eight for FORTITUDE

Lord, give me the <u>fortitude</u> to stand up against temptation and grant me the persistence to hang in there when the going gets really tough.

Day Nine for TEMPERANCE

Lord, help me to practice <u>temperance</u> in all ways for the good of both my spiritual and my physical welfare.

To report favors obtained through the intercession of Father Damien, to obtain more information, novenas, pictures, prayer cards or relics, the following sources may be contacted:

Damien Museum and Archives
130 Ohua Avenue
Honolulu, HI 96815
Phone (808) 923-2690

Rev. Father Matthew Sullivan SS.CC.
Director, Father Damien's Cause
3 Adams Street
Fairhaven, MA 02719
Phone (508) 999-0400

Rev. Father Ron Gronowski
St. Michael the Archangel Church
PO Box 1059
Kailua-Kona, HI 96745
(808) 326-7771

Rev. Father Charles Oyabu, S.M., Pastor
Holy Rosary Church
Father Damien Memorial
954 Baldwin Avenue
Paia, Maui, HI 96779
Phone (808) 579-9551

Rev. Father Arsene Daenen, SS.CC.
Kalaupapa Settlement
Kalaupapa, HI 96742

Bibliography

* Bunson, Mararet R. *Father Damien, The Man and His Era,* Huntington, Ind., Our Sunday Visitor, C 1989

* Daughters of St. Paul. *No Greater Love: The Life of Fr. Damien of Molokai,* Boston, Daughters of St. Paul, C 1979

* Daws, Gavan. *Holy Man,* Father Damien of Molokai, Honolulu University of Hawaii Pr. C 1973

* Englebert, Omer. *The Hero of Molokai: Father Damien, Apostle of the Lepers,* (tr. By Benjamin Crawford) Boston, Daughters of St. Paul. C 1963

* Farrow, John. *Damien the Leper,* N.Y. Sheed and Ward, C 1937

* Jourdain, SS.CC., Vital. *The Heart of Father Damien, 1840-1889.* Milwaukee, Bruce Pub. Co., C 1955

* Law, Anwei V.S. and Richard A. Wisniewski. *Kalaupapa and the Legacy of Father Damien,* Honolulu, Pacific Printers, Inc. C 1988

* Myers, Rawley. *People Who Loved,* Vol. II Notre Dame, Inc. Fides Publishers, Inc. C 1971

* Sheehan, Arthur and Elizabeth. *Father Damien and the Bells,* N.Y. Guild Pr. C 1962

* Various pamphlets from the Damien Museum in Honolulu, HI

* Article in *Christian Renewal News, Mar. 1994--Damien of Molokai, Servant of God-Servant of Humanity.*

Acknowledgments

Thanks are due to the following for kind support, encouragement, helpful reference materials and prayers:

My Grand Rapids Dominican Sisters.
Marie Sivak, long time friend since Library School days.
Dr. Frederick O'Hara, Professor Emeritus of Palmer School of Library Information Science, Long Island University, once my instructor at Western Michigan University.
Art Fettig, President of Growth Unlimited, who wouldn't let me give up and sent books and other reference materials from Hawaii.

For permissions, encouragement and prayers: **Sister Carmelita Murphy, O.P.,** Prioress General (1988-1994) **Sister Barbara Hansen, O.P.,** present Prioress General of the Grand Rapids Dominicans.

For reading and critiquing the manuscript: **Sister Jean Milhaupt, O.P.,** Professor of English at Aquinas College, Grand Rapids, MI.

For suggestions and recommendations: **Sister Judith Kirt, O.P., Sister Jean Anita Williams, O.P.,** and **Sister Malvena Nadon, O.P.**

To the Sisters I live with for good-natured tolerance while I struggled toward the completion of this book: **Sister Theresa Pelky, R.S.M., Sister Judith Kirt, O.P. and Sister Marie Eugene Charboneau, O.P.**

For saving me many hours of precious time, by producing the final typewritten manuscript: My niece, **Marlette Reibel** and her husband, **Lee Reibel**

For excellent artistic input: **Bill Tatroe**

For title and phrasal additions, design, layout and typesetting, which she made a beautiful labor of love: **Paula Hopkins**

Sister Mary Pelagia
Litkowski, O.P.

About The Author

Florence Irene Litkowski was born to Peter and Florence Litkowski in Saginaw, Michigan where she was educated in Saginaw elementary public schools and in St. Joseph High School taught by the Grand Rapids Dominican Sisters. She made profession as a Dominican Sister at Marywood in Grand Rapids, Michigan in 1934, receiving the name of Sister Mary Pelagia of Our Lady of Lourdes. She taught in Catholic elementary schools in Michigan until 1961 when she received a Master's Degree in librarianship from Western Michigan University in Kalamazoo, Michigan. She has served as librarian in several parochial schools in Michigan.

In September, 1988 she was the recipient of the Michigan Catholic Library Association's Gabriel Richard Award for meritorious contributions to Catholic librarianship.

In 1989 she received the Annual Kateri Tekakwitha Award for her book about Kateri.

Her life-long hobby has been writing plays, letters and newspaper articles. After hearing a homily about Father Damien and the possibility of his becoming the patron of those suffering from AIDS (the leprosy of today) she was inspired to write about him for the young and not so young.

This is the fourth book, the first three being, Friend To All: St. John Neumann CSSR, Kateri Tekakwitha, Joyful Lover and Margaret of Castello: Unwanted One.

Presently Sister is volunteer librarian at St. Michael Elementary School in Brunswick/Fremont. She resides at St. Michael Convent, 10250 N. Maple Island Road, Fremont, MI 49412-9116.

Other Books

by Sister Mary Pelagia Litkowski

Friend to All:
St. John Nepomecene Neumann, CSSR
Fourth Bishop of Philadelphia, St. John Neumann
spent much of his time establishing schools and
earning the title *The Children's Bishop*. This is the
story of his remarkable life. *64 Pages $3.95*

Kateri Tekakwitha:
Joyful Lover
Native American Kateri Tekakwitha's
life is a model for today's youth. She
represents womanhood, deprived
minorities and the handicapped as well.
This inspiring story is a must for children.
64 Pages $5.95

Margaret of Castello:
Unwanted One
Born blind, a hunchback cripple, Margaret
of Castello was abandoned by her parents
in a strange city. This fantastic story will
inspire children to face their daily challenges
and serve the Lord. *64 Pages $5.95*

Available From:

Sister Mary Pelagia Litkowski, O.P.
10250 N. Maple Island Road
Fremont, MI 49412-9116